LIFE IN GOD'S
PRESENCE

A simple approach to prayer

LIFE IN GOD'S
PRESENCE

A simple approach to prayer

by a Carthusian

Scepter

With ecclesiastical approval

Copyright © 2011, Scepter Publishers, Inc.

A translation by Bernard Browne of *Das Leben in Gott: Einführung ins Geistliche Leben Mit einem Vorwort* von Klaus Martin Becker.

Original work is © 2005 Adamas Verlag, GmbH, Köln. Published with permission.

Scepter Publishers, Inc.
P.O. Box 211, New York, N.Y. 10018
www.scepterpublishers.org

Text design by Carol Sawyer/Rose Design

Printed in the United States of America

ISBN: 978 1 59417 144 4

CONTENTS

༄

CHAPTER 3

The Spirit of the Gospel   33

FOREWORD TO THE NEW EDITION

> The kingdom of heaven is like a merchant in search of fine pearls, who, on finding one pearl of great value, went and sold all that he had and bought it.
>
> — Mt 13:45–46

Could we find a more precious pearl than life in God, in the Triune God? In him alone do we find fulfillment. This is what we are created for.

A little book is not the Kingdom of Heaven. But it can be a precious pearl just the same, one in whose gleam we can discover the Kingdom of God within us (cf. Lk 17:21). It's worthwhile acquiring this precious pearl. Its riches are revealed only to one who reads carefully, considers, and prays about what is here presented in simple, clear words.

This little book from the pen of a nameless, silent Carthusian takes its teachings from the fountain of Christian experience from earliest times up to our own day. The fountain is timeless, or reaches across time. The one who wrote this book gives us "living water . . . welling up [in us] to eternal life" (Jn 4:14). One can't really call the writer an *author*, for he was, in all probability, fully convinced of the words of St. Paul: "What have you that you did not receive?" (1 Cor 4:7).

Thankfully, these handwritten words from the early part of the twentieth century were preserved and published by Father Friedrich Kronseder S.J., apparently after being polished by a mystical writer of the Carthusian order whose name *is* known, Father Anton Jans.[1] Father Jans, as Kronseder reports, "highly esteemed the hand-written original of this book and left it to his parents as a remembrance."[2] Whether, and to what extent, Father Jans had a hand in the writing remains unknown, but in the long run it really doesn't matter. It is part of the personal and collective humility of the spirit of St. Bruno, the founder of the Carthusian Order, to remain anonymous, understanding in this way the words that St. Paul wrote to the Colossians: "For you have died, and your life is hid with Christ in God" (Col 3:3).

---

1. Cf. Martin Grabmann: *Pater Anton Jans—Ein Mystikerleben der Gegenwart*, Munich, 1934.
2. From the Foreword to this book published by Fr. Friedrich Kronseder, under the title: *Das Leben in Gott—Einführung ins geistliche Leben*, Regensburg, 1935, pp. 7–8.

This book is about something, namely life in God, which has matured in Christian experience from earliest times. Here we find it expressed and written down, offering us a foundation on which safely to build the house of our spiritual life without danger that some storm might bring it down. This firm foundation is offered to every individual, whether in the world—which the laity are called to permeate with the light of the Gospel and form in accordance with God's will, as the Second Vatican Council teaches (*Lumen Gentium*, 31f)—or in "separation from the world"—the vocation of members of religious orders, as the Council also teaches (*Perfectae Caritatis*, 5); or finally as a priest, who in the service of the Word and of the sacraments, stand in the person of Christ the Head of the Church (*Presbyterorum Ordinis*, 2). The difference lies in the particular vocation of each person. The plan is the same: life in God. The structure of the building, on the other hand, may differ substantially. There is a legitimate freedom here, a catholic fullness and broadness of scope.

Life in God, the structural plan of the spiritual life, means taking part in the inner life of the Triune God, it means becoming holy oneself. God the Father, in Christ his Son, "chose us in him before the foundation of the world, that we should be holy and blameless before him. He destined us in love to be his sons through Jesus Christ, according to the purpose of his will, to the praise of his glorious grace which he freely bestowed on us in the Beloved" (Eph 1:4–6). Everyone is called to this holiness. The "universal call to holiness" was one of the main themes of the Second Vatican Council (*Lumen Gentium*, Chapter 5).

"A secret, an open secret," said St. Josemaría Escrivá, "these world crises are crises of saints. God wants a handful of men 'of his own' in every human activity. And then . . . *pax Christi in regno Christi*— the peace of Christ in the kingdom of Christ."[3]

This appeal shows us the urgency of finding a workable building plan for our personal holiness. Such a plan is presented in this book.

I would like to thank all of those responsible for making this new edition possible: especially the Carthusians of the Marienau monastery and Adamas Verlag.

Klaus M. Becker
Cologne, Germany

---

3. St. Josemaría Escrivá, *The Way*, no. 301.

INTRODUCTION

Jesus Christ said: "The Kingdom of God is within you."

— *Lk 17:21*

Within us not just in any way at all, but deep in our being: "If a man loves me, he will keep my word, and my Father will love him, and we will come to him and make our home with him" (Jn 14:23).

Unfortunately, we think of this truth too little. Many souls honestly strive to live an ever more spotless life. But only a few choose the faith as their sure leader, draw strength from hope, let themselves be completely enkindled by love, and thus have a perfect participation in the life that Jesus brought us.

We live surrounded by proofs of God's love. It is not God who hinders us from living closely united with him from today on. We simply have to want to live this supernatural life in God with our whole will. We know the guidelines; the path lies open before us. It is up to us to take that path. If we don't, it's our own fault.

But let's admit it, "the sons of this world are wiser in dealing with their own generation than the sons of light" (Lk 16:8). We bear within us a precious treasure of infinite value—sanctifying grace. But we fail to appreciate it, and thus make it unfruitful. Didn't our Lord hint at this, when he spoke in a parable about the talent that the unfaithful servant buried in the earth and left there (Mt 25:18)?

Jesus is not satisfied with just offering us this treasure of a deep communion of love. He urges us forcefully; he almost forces us to accept him. He behaves toward us as was done with those poor and crippled people in the Gospel whom the lord called to the divine feast and did not leave free to refuse the invitation: "*compelle intrare*"—"force them to come" (Lk 14:23).

Let us accept the invitation he offers us in his goodness and pray to God from now on with the Church: "Almighty and ever-living God, strengthen our faith, hope, and love" (opening prayer of the thirtieth Sunday in ordinary time).

Let us not be satisfied with just beginning and ending our day's work with a few short prayers. Such isolated exercises do not constitute a life. A life consists of a persistent, lasting activity. Jesus himself wants to be our life. "I am the Life" (Jn 11:25).

We should always, without interruption, be united with God. It's not a matter of attending to God with this or that act of devotion. He wants all of us. He asks for all of our time, all of our strength, our whole soul. In return he gives us the possibility of beginning eternal life here on earth.

Let us follow the call of our Master so that we can breathe the wonderfully pure, clear air of everlasting truth and love.

To lead souls into that supernatural world, we will sketch out in the following pages a simple, practical way of meditation that will enable souls to make an uninterrupted prayer of their whole day's work in accord with the words of the Gospel: "they ought always to pray and not lose heart" (Lk 18:1).

But before we describe this way of meditating, we will present the foundations on which it rests. Following this, we will show that these truths and their consequences are clearly presented in the Gospels and are to be found in the words of Jesus himself.

CHAPTER 1

General Principles

A Supernatural Goal

When we look back at our spiritual life up to now, we are amazed—perhaps even dismayed—by our slow progress or maybe by our lack of any progress. Why, after a number of years of trying to live a spiritual life, are we still reproaching ourselves for the same weaknesses and failures? Haven't we from the very beginning been neglecting the most important thing, been following the wrong path?

There is only one door that leads into the kingdom of divine life. Vain are our efforts to get there some other way. Insuperable obstacles arise in our path. We resemble not very skillful thieves, who try stealthily, but in vain, to find their way into a well-guarded house. "He who does not enter . . . by the door but climbs in by another way, that man is a thief and a robber" (Jn 10:1).

This solitary door is Christ: "I am the door" (Jn 10:7). It is faith in him. "Whoever believes in me has eternal life" (Jn 6:47). But only a faith vivified by love, which is clothed with strength from above (Lk 24:49), inflames one to an active love, and allows this love more and more to shine forth according to the model of divine Love.

An asceticism that strives only for the perfection of one's own self or ego is to be rejected as egocentric and therefore completely inadequate. Its results would always be very poor and its fruits deceptive. If what one sows is only human, what one reaps will also be only human.

Christian asceticism instead rests completely on a divine principle, a principle that vivifies, inspires, and leads one to one's goal: "You shall love the Lord your God with all your heart, and with all your soul, and with all your might" (Deut 6:5 and Mt 22:37). That's the epitome and high point of the Old Testament Law. The New Testament took over this first and highest commandment, perfected it, and proclaimed it as generally binding throughout the world in all its radiant simplicity and electrifying power.

Right at the beginning of their spiritual lives, souls should be steered to this sea of love, to God. One who turns elsewhere does not understand the deepest meaning of Christianity. He will naturally be drawn back to egoistic strivings and goals. He will build like the architects of the pagan antiquity and today upon a vainglorious heroism, and nurture a barren culture springing out of his own ego.

How differently our lives will appear when we once and for all are convinced of the truth of the words of our heavenly Master: "Apart from me you can do nothing" (Jn 15:5). "Lord, send forth your Spirit, thus was all created; and you shall renew the face of the earth" (Ps 104:30). Filled with this truth of love, we will strive to practice not just this virtue or that but all the virtues without exception, in the conviction that God must be not only the goal but the source of all of our willing and doing as well.

We will use all our strength as if the success of all depended on us alone, but will remain humble in regard to our progress and trusting despite our failures. Deeply conscious of the fact that we ourselves are nothing, and by ourselves can do nothing, but that through Christ we are all-powerful—"I can do all things in him who strengthens me" (Phil 4:13)—we will be neither discouraged by our failures nor proud of any acts of virtue that we succeed in performing through God's grace.

Yes, we dare to say even more. For a soul who has experienced his or her own helplessness on the one hand and God's omnipotence on the other, failings and weaknesses are not hindrances any more, but, on the contrary, means for progress. For they offer us an opportunity, by awakening an heroic act of virtue, to increase our faith in the goodness and mercy of God and to throw ourselves trustingly into his arms once again; since, precisely in our failures, we have experienced and proven that everything falls apart that does not clearly and purely have God as its goal. "I will all the more gladly boast of my weaknesses, that the power of Christ may be shown in me" (2 Cor 12:9).

As soon as, taught by such experiences, we begin to rely only on God and not on ourselves, we will start to walk with giant steps on the path of love. The love of God will make our willing purer and simpler, it will direct our actions more and more to their goal, until it has fully saturated and formed our being and life.

In this earnest and upright striving to live according to the teaching of the Gospels, we will then let ourselves be led solely by motivations of faith and love. We will succeed in this only if, from the beginning of our spiritual lives, we let ourselves be led and governed by these divine virtues, for supernatural fruit cannot be derived from natural principles. How can we hope to attain our spiritual goal by our own unaided efforts if we, as St. Paul says, cannot even speak the name of the Lord without the help of grace?

Certainly reforming the life of the "old man" requires strong work on our will. But when is the will's strength more determined and effective: when it springs only from the conclusions of reason or when it strives for its goal motivated by the superior motives of crystal clear faith and pure love? The answer seems clear. So in forming, developing, and deploying our inner lives, we should use as much as possible the light and strength provided by the divine virtues. From the very beginning everyone, with all the strength of our being and God's grace, we must focus upon a clear goal: that realm of the interior life that is union with God.

This kingdom of Christ is open to everyone. Indeed, it is the express wish of our Lord that we take possession of it. "Abide in me and I in you" (Jn 15:4). Let us respond to his call this very day and begin to live by faith! "He who through faith is righteous shall live" (Rom 1:17).

A Life Based on Faith

Belief in God's real presence around and within us is first and most important. The activity of our will and understanding should rise to the level of that true life for which God has created us. This act of faith, which transforms and divinizes our whole life at once, is very difficult for our human nature. It requires a high level of strength, which we are not capable of unless God supports our striving with his prevenient and helping grace. Unable by our own ability to awaken this first act of faith, we ask like the father of the sick boy in the Gospel: "Lord, help my unbelief" (Mk 9:24).

Through faith we receive the sure guarantee of the divine promises. "I will betroth you to me in faithfulness" (Hos 2:20). During our temporal, material lives on earth, he allows us to walk in his holy darkness. "For we walk by faith, not by sight" (2 Cor 5:7). From start to finish let us follow this way and never turn from it satisfied too easily by that human wisdom that soon disappoints.

Faith is a strict but unfailing leader. It knows nothing of concessions and calculations: it doesn't mull over the difficulties in the battle against self-love. Behind the veil of the visible it detects the eternal truth, the victory of Jesus: "This is the victory that overcomes the world, our faith" (1 Jn 5:4). Faith creates that supernatural cosmos and that sphere of life saturated with divine strength, in which alone true love can flourish. It hopes despite all human hindrances, which want to cripple or destroy its momentum, as St. Paul says of the Patriarch Abraham: "In hope he believed against hope. . . . No distrust made him waver . . . but he grew strong in his faith" (Rom 4:18–20).

All of our Lord's teaching rests on faith. To doubt means to become weak, "O man of little faith, why did you doubt?" (Mt 14:31). From faith comes salvation. Christ himself attributed his miracles to the faith of the sick people whom he healed.

A spark of faith is enough to change the whole world supernaturally: "If you have faith as [great as] a grain of mustard seed . . ." (Mt 17:20). "All things are possible to him who believes" (Mk 9:23).

"If you abide in me, and my words abide in you, ask whatever you will, and it shall be done for you" (Jn 15:7).

We place these facts at the beginning of our discussion to indicate the markers along the way that we must follow in order to follow our divine Savior with determined boldness and high-minded trust. For trust in God is the decisive turning point in the spiritual life.

We will seek in the following presentation to sketch the essential guidelines for the interior life and to lay out the principles on which it rests. We have already indicated the starting point: faith.

When divine grace completes its work in us, a supernatural assurance will rule over our soul and transform it into a temple of love in accordance with the words of St. Paul: "faith . . . works by charity" (Gal 5:6), and "that Christ may dwell in your hearts through faith; that you may . . . know the love of Christ which surpasses knowledge" (cf. Eph 3:17–19).

The Natural Presence of God in All Things

In order to understand the supernatural presence of God better, let us remind ourselves first of all, of how God is naturally present.

God is everywhere. We think much too little about this very simple truth. But it can give our lives a whole new direction; indeed it can even transform them, if we let ourselves be more and more infused with this awareness.

We often struggle with our imagination to picture a God who is very far away. Our prayer necessarily suffers from this. God is a spirit—"*Spiritus est Deus*" (Jn 4:24)—a spirit who is not tied to space and place, but rather permeates everything that there is. Those who truly pray, then, pray to God "in spirit and in truth" (Jn 4:24). Just think of the words of St. Paul: "In him we live and move and have our being" (Acts 17:28).

We should begin the spiritual life by grasping this lofty truth as deeply as possible. The impact of keeping the thought of the immediate and universal presence of God vividly before us can hardly be exaggerated.

Pure reason, aside from any supernatural revelation, tells us that God knows us perfectly and constantly sees us, since he knows and sees everything. "Whither shall I go from thy Spirit? Or whither shall I flee from thy presence? If I ascend to heaven, thou art there! If I make my bed in Sheol, thou art there" (Ps 139:7–8).

But God doesn't just watch over us with his gaze, he also orders and directs everything that we do. "For God is at work in you, both to will and to work" (Phil 2:13). I would not be able to move my little finger, if God were not substantially present and active in me. There is nothing, absolutely nothing, which can remove itself from this presence. Even in the case of a "sinful" act, God is present; otherwise it would not be possible to carry out the act. The only thing that does not come from God is the depravity of the will through which the act becomes a sin. Since God is the first and only source of all things, we cannot do the slightest thing alone. He would cease to be God if this were otherwise. "If I take the wings of the morning and dwell in the uttermost parts of the sea, even there thy hand shall lead me, and thy right hand shall hold me" (Ps 139:9–10).

But still more! It is not enough that God leads his creatures and guides their activity. As the one ultimate cause of all beings, he has also to keep them in existence and at every moment give them their essence and existence anew. The whole universe, and we with it, would fall into nothingness like a dream if this divine activity were to cease for a single second. When one has once grasped the absolute necessity of this divine presence, he will see a very special greatness—the greatness of God—shining forth from even the most unlikely object. For the Almighty himself, and he alone, preserves this little thing from nothingness by his presence.

We look upon shadows as the least substantial of all realities. In comparison to our own being, our shadow is nothing. But we have still less reality in comparison with God who is within us. Measured against the divine reality, we are not even shadow images.

The Supernatural Presence of God in Souls

God then is present in the stone that lies before us, making it be the stone it is by his direct action.

But in his infinite goodness God made beings "according to his image and likeness" (Gen 1:26ff). These through grace were raised above their nature, and stand much closer to him than those substances of a lesser order, to which he merely gave their natural being.

God is pure spirit. Since he created beings "in his image," he gave them understanding and will as well, so that he could be in them not only as he is in all other things, but in order to raise them to the supernatural state of grace and to share with them his being as he is himself. God is in material things in such a way that he gives them their natural being; but in creatures endowed with understanding, he wanted, out of free generosity, to be present in such a way that he not only gave them their natural being, but his own nature. He wishes thus to raise them to himself, to unite them directly with himself through the bond of love and to divinize them.

"*Efficiamini divinae consortes naturae*—That you may become partakers of the divine nature" (2 Pet 1:4).

God was not required to give himself in this wonderful way. But he is goodness itself, and it is proper to this goodness to share itself and to pour itself forth. God is like a fire that refuses to be quenched and sets fire to all that is flammable. "For the Lord your God is a devouring fire" (Deut 4:24).

The Eternal Word became man, to share this fire with us. "I came to cast fire upon the earth; and would that it were already kindled!" (Lk 12:49).

Christ suffered and died to win this grace for us, to make us receptive to this divine firebrand. And we will be such, insofar as we distance ourselves from whatever stands in the way of this divine work within us. The worst of these hindrances is sin. "If a man loves me, he will keep my word, and we will come to him and make our home with him" (Jn 14:23).

Our divine Savior has not only united us with the life stream of his eternal Father, but he wanted to continue to live with us in the Holy Eucharist, constantly to increase this divine life in us. "No one comes to the Father but by me" (Jn 14:6). Jesus is the way, and indeed the only way, to the Father. To want to reach divine life without him is presumption and self-deception. The more we approach his holy humanity through love, the more lovingly we consider and meditate on his example, the more strongly will divine life grow in us and stream through us. "I came that they may have life, and have it abundantly" (Jn 10:10).

Mortal Sin Robs the Soul of the Divine Presence

We are destined to a deep inner union with God. "I have loved you with an everlasting love" (Jer 31:3). This bond of man with his Creator was first realized when God raised our first parents to the supernatural order. But through sin Adam and Eve rebelled against God, and the bond between heaven and earth, between God and man, was broken. It required a God-man to restore this unity, to bridge the chasm between fallen man and God. Through the merits of his holy suffering and death we can now be children of God again and live the divine life.

In Baptism we are given a share in this life, while those who have unfortunately lost it can regain it through perfect contrition or through the holy Sacrament of Reconciliation. In this way Christ grants us the divine life once more through a mystical purification in his precious Blood.

If only we could see the importance to us of this flight from sin! It's a matter of not losing the most precious gift that was ever given to man. "If you [only] knew the gift of God!" (Jn 4:10). May these words of Christ to the Samaritan woman never be a reproach to us.

All suffering and misfortune put together are nothing in comparison to a single sin, since a single serious sin robs us of divine life. In order to grasp the hideousness of sin just a little bit, let's use the following comparison: What Catholic would have the audacity secretly to break into a church, to break open the tabernacle, and to throw the sacred Hosts on the floor and desecrate them? Could we ever do such a thing, would we have the outrageous audacity for that? Surely not. Not even the most lukewarm Catholic would dare to perform such a sacrilege against the Body of our Lord. But what do we do through sin? We throw God out of our hearts and hand them over to occupation by Satan.

How is God Present in Us in a Supernatural Way?

We know that in God there is one nature in three Divine Persons. From eternity the Father generated the Son, his perfect image. He did not generate him just once at the beginning of time, but this act takes place in his eternal present: It is being carried out at this moment as it was before the beginning of time. He loves this divine Son who is consubstantial with him with a love of total self-giving. And the Son loves the Father in the same way. The Holy Spirit proceeds from the Father and the Son in this mutual love.

Inasmuch as someone is in the state of grace, he or she can here and now possess the divine life that will someday be the fulfillment of happiness. In this august state, the Father generates the Son in one's grace-filled soul, and the Father and Son breathe forth the Holy Spirit in that wonderful, mysterious unity of love.

Up to this time have we sufficiently taken note of and reflected on this most joyous and shining of truths?

Many of us are accustomed to wear or carry with us scapulars, medals, relics or other pious objects. We believe, and rightly so, that we possess a precious treasure in them.

But we have within us the living God himself, the only goal of all things, the highest reality . . . and we don't think about it! Accustomed though we are to having rosaries always with us, we so easily forget about the Holy of Holies, God, our Creator, Sustainer, Savior, the highest and most lovable good that we can bear within us. How sad! Through this supernatural presence of God in our soul, we have become in the full sense of the words Christ-bearers, God-bearers. Souls like that are the objects of an eternal movement of love that proceeds from God. If anywhere, here is the place to remind ourselves of the words of St. Leo the Great: "*Agnosce Christiane, dignitatem tuam*—Recognize, O Christian, your dignity!"

From this so simple, yet luminous truth comes a conclusion of the greatest importance: Our lives are fully transformed as soon as we allow the divine indwelling, the presence of God in us, to have its way, without resistance from us.

Life in God's Presence through Faith, Hope, and Love

How do we achieve this transformation of our lives?

God would not be the eternal goodness and wisdom if he did not—along with his courting of our love—give us the means to this unity with him. These means, which bring us with certainty into direct relationship with God, are the three theological virtues and the gifts of the Holy Spirit that accompany them.

By faith we affirm the truth of the divine life that has been promised to us. Through love we possess it. Hope gives us the certainty that with the help of grace we will grow in this life and finally possess it perfectly and unendingly in heaven.

In this activity of the three theological virtues is the substance of every deep and sincere prayer. We can carry on a conversation directly with God in the innocence and simplicity of our souls. "*In simplicitate cordis quaerite illum*—Seek him with simplicity of heart" (Wis 1:1). Why should we direct our first to this, then to that and thus split it up? Why should we philosophize about God, tiring intellect, will, and imagination through tedious presentations of pictures and scenes, when we can remain, through simple meditation in the spirit of faith and love, close to the source of life and thus connect ourselves directly with God?

Our divine Savior himself demands this simplicity of us: "Be as simple as doves" (Mt 10:16). God himself is, after all, also simplicity. The more innocent and simple we are, the more is our gaze directed upon him and so much the nearer we come to him; while on the contrary, the more complicated we are, the more we distance ourselves from him.

Simplicity is the atmosphere of God. We know that God, our Father, is present in us. Does a child, if it wants to speak with its Father, consult a book to see what subject of conversation it should choose, what forms of speech it should use? No, the child speaks directly and simply, it does not think about how to frame its sentences, nor does it consider outward forms. Let's do the same in *our* dealings with our heavenly Father. Our Savior told us, didn't he: "Unless you turn and become like children, you will never enter the kingdom of heaven" (Mt 18:3).

Is a mother ever tired of hearing her child say, "Mother, I love you"? It's the same with God: the more childlike our prayer is, the more it pleases him. He himself chose as the most beautiful of all names that of "Father." "God has sent the Spirit of his Son into our hearts, crying, '*Abba*! Father!'" (Gal 4:6).

Our prayer then should be very simple, as simple as possible. We should awaken with the whole soul acts of faith, hope, and love. There is no better, more august, surer, and more commendable way of praying.

CHAPTER 2

Ways of Meditating

Here is an example of this way of praying and meditating.

An Act of Faith

My God, I believe everything that you have revealed and presented to us for belief through your Church. I believe that you are here in me—in *me*, a poor nothing. Yes, if only I were just nothing! But I have offended you; I have rebelled against your will. Therefore I am less than nothing. . . . The animals have not offended you as I have, and nevertheless you condescend to live in me. In consideration of such goodness I should be very contrite, and instead I am puffed up with pride and filled with self-love.

My God, in spite of all this I pray to you, who are within me. . . . I believe steadfastly that you are present in me. Give me your grace, to attain such a strong and true faith that nothing can ever separate me from you. Like the blind man in the gospel I ask you: "Lord, that I might see!" (Lk 18:41; Mk 10:51). Let the scales fall from my eyes; heal my blindness. And in the light of your presence, I will learn to know myself and find and love you in all things, and all things in you.

An Act of Hope

My God, I hope in you, the unending Goodness, who wants to set up your dwelling place in me. . . . But how can I dare to hope in you, I who am such a miserable, such a deeply stained, ungrateful creature. I should really say with St. Peter, "Depart from me, for I am a sinful man, O Lord" (Lk 5:8).

But please don't, my God! I know that you yourself said that you had not come for the just, who did not need a physician or savior, but for sinners. And so I will use the title "sinner" as a basis for my trust. I can and must hope in you, just because I am a sinner.

But I'm not satisfied with just hoping. Through your grace I have a strong trust, even a certainty, that you are always with me and in me and you want to stay there, as St. Paul says: "If God is for us, who is against us? I am sure that neither death, nor life . . . nor anything else in all creation, will be able to separate us from the love of God in Christ Jesus our Lord" (Rom 8:31, 38).

From now on I feel myself secure in you, my God, and know myself to be protected by you. I fear nothing at all any more: the world, hell, the flesh may rise up against me, what is that to me! They are powerless, for you are with me, "O Lord, my strength. The Lord is my rock, and my fortress . . . my shield, and the horn of my salvation, my stronghold" (Ps 18: 2–3). You are my Emmanuel, my "God with us," my God and my all.

An Act of Love

How can I say that I love you, my God, when I insult you so often and so deeply? My life should be an unbroken, direct, self-less love for you, for you have created me only to love you. But I see only a few moments in my life that were dedicated to your love. And even there the noblest deeds and the purest feelings were troubled by self-love and self-seeking. What ingratitude to you who ceaselessly pursue me with your love. . . .

But I still surrender myself to you today, my God, and want to confess: Lord, you have conquered! Since you have died on the Cross out of love for me, I want at least to live out of love for you. And if I still can't say that I really love you, at least I do long to love you and to prove this love by deeds.

This practice of the three supernatural virtues in no way excludes other attitudes and feelings toward God. One can, in between, consider humility, faith, abandonment, adoration, all of which we need in order to acquire virtues and to get rid of our failings. When we constantly and earnestly converse with God in this way, we will surely make true progress in spiritual life.

When rightly disposed to speak from the fullness of our hearts, we shall find it easy to fill the time we have set aside for meditation with such acts of virtue. Our prayer then is done very well.

If, on the other hand, we are dry and cold and can't find any words, having made acts of faith, hope, and love, we then can take up a book and use its words to enliven once more the soul's contact with God. But if we want this reading to become meditation, we must not read page after page quickly, but instead stop at each sentence and make it vivid and personal, so that one speaks to God with each word or phrase, applies it to one's own soul and draws out personal resolutions. "You, my God . . . I, your creature!"

So, for instance, the words "Our Savior suffered for mankind" are at once translated into "You, my Savior, suffered for me." This way of personalizing general thoughts enables us to personalize what we say in our conversation with God. It protects us against the danger of losing ourselves in speculative, merely theoretical considerations. Instead of that, one might speak with God, for example, in the following way: Who are you, who have come down from heaven . . . why did you come to this earth . . . why did you suffer . . . and what did you suffer, and for whom?

You, my God, have taken on a human form, in order to suffer . . . to suffer immeasurably, for ungrateful me . . . and you died on a Cross and asked your heavenly Father to forgive me, who drove you to the Cross . . . ! And I won't tolerate the slightest unpleasantness although I know that I deserve to suffer much, much more.

No, from now on, my beloved Savior, I will not be cold and indifferent toward you. Your cry from the cross should be sounding always in my soul: "I thirst" (Jn 19:28). Yes, you suffered thirst, bodily thirst, through the tortures that my sins caused you. But above all you suffered thirst for love, because up till now you have not received from me any of the true, noble, upright, and self-sacrificing love you wished. Therefore I resolve from this time on to give you all of my love and only love. Everything I suffer now and in the future shall be united interiorly with your suffering and suffered only for love of you.

The Role of Imagination

One might suggest that there is too little of one's imagination in this kind of meditation. Actually, that is just what we want.

The work of the imagination is a purely human activity, and therefore it is not prayer. That's the first reason why we want to reduce it to what is essential. Of course, through the influence of grace this subordinate activity is ennobled and can be directed toward a supernatural goal. But despite this, it is still true that the power of the imagination, like any capacity related to sensation tires quickly and grows weary of its object. To call forth fantasy pictures and hold on to them is too strenuous a task for one to be able to continue with it for any length of time. Consequently, we can't obtain any substantial or even notable part of our prayer life from this source since, according to the demands of the Gospel, prayer should be simple and continual. "*Oportet semper orare et non deficere*—One ought always to pray and not lose heart" (Lk 18:1).

Besides, the imagination is not able to get in touch with the supernatural realities. These are only accessible through pure faith. One can at most play with the shadows, with the veils of these invisible realities, while we can reach immediate, interior connection with them through the divine virtues.

Does that mean we must exclude any pictorial images from our prayer? No, for that is impossible; but one should only make use of them to the extent that it is necessary and beneficial, no more.

You are considering, for example, the suffering of our Lord. You first seek him within you. You turn to him, present to you through his divinity. The imagination may then awaken in you, for example, with the help of a crucifix, an image of what he suffered on the cross for us. But one is always conscious that he is present in one's heart.

This procedure does not in any way weaken the intimacy, the liveliness, and the strength of your disposition and feelings toward our divine Savior. On the contrary! For pure faith gives our feelings life and depth, and teaches us that just as our present sins truly hurt Jesus during his Passion, so our present acts of love in like manner truly comforted him.

How heartening it is for a loving soul to know that through her love she can and should comfort our divine Savior in the Garden of Gethsemane, where he is saddened unto death and abandoned by everyone. And that is no flight of fancy or illusion, but unadulterated, sublime truth and a reality of faith.

Practical Results of Meditation

The entire life of Christian virtue comes into definitive focus as meditation and spiritual reading point us at length to the conclusion that God is everything and we are nothing. "My God, you are unlimited being, I am nothing; you are beauty, I am misery and ugliness; you are splendor, I am so sinful."

In this way we shall succeed more and more in attaining the state of contrition, which is the necessary foundation of a serious interior life. We shall come to the conviction that we are completely incapable of doing what is good and that the only way to attain true life is to act more through God and for God.

Let us carry with us from every meditation a solid resolution to keep ourselves in the presence of God during the day ahead and frequently to renew this simple act. We recollect ourselves quietly, retreat into our interior, and here greet God, who is present, through acts of faith, of hope, and of love. This life and this communication with God will enable us continually to avoid sin, and quickly and surely make progress in virtue.

Never forget that the moral virtues cannot be ends in themselves. No created thing is there for its own sake and is itself an end. And this includes virtue. To practice virtue just for the sake of virtue is a narrow and paltry ideal, discouraging because of the impossibility of realizing it. Whoever flees the world for the sake of a pathetic happiness and believes himself or herself perfect on this account, or else remains in the world so as to struggle against it, thereby feeling he or she is a conqueror and gaining a reputation, will never attain true nobility but only the outward appearance of virtuousness. Such people will never rise above the natural level of "good works," performed with the aim of raising themselves above themselves. The goal of the Christian is supernatural and far beyond the reach of any merely human tactic or maneuver. We can attain it only through divine love, which constantly grows through interior contact with God and, to the extent it grows, causes all the other virtues to grow.

"One Must Always Pray"

Repeating as often as possible during the day the essential act of recollection, we each time reawaken and revivify within us the spirit of prayer. The words of St. John become a shining star and bright light in our life: "God is love, and he who abides in love abides in God, and God abides in him" (1 Jn 4:16). As a result we experience and put into effect that other point of the same apostle: "No one born of God commits sin; for God's nature abides in him" (1 Jn 3:9).

Nothing is easier than from time to time to free ourselves—even if only for a few seconds—from the concerns and activities of daily life, to unite ourselves with God. "It is good to be near God; I have made the Lord God my refuge" (Ps 73:28). At every moment I can speak with him, there is no need for words. A short glance within me, a greeting, an act of love, of trust, a request for light and strength, according to circumstances and needs, is enough. "I remembered God, and was gladdened" (cf. Ps 76). And so I gradually create an inner solitude in which I can always listen closely to the voice of my beloved, who himself has promised me this closeness: "I will . . . bring her into the wilderness, and speak tenderly to her" (Hos 2:14).

With ever-greater faithfulness I will make an effort to listen to this voice and always joyfully to carry out what he wants of me. "Let me hear what God the Lord will speak" (Ps 85:8). When difficulties confront me, I will take refuge in him. In him I find light and strength, with him I share my joy. In a word: He takes first place in my thoughts and my deeds. My whole life, previously centered only upon my own ego, will from now on find its entire meaning and purpose in him alone.

I do all of this without great intellectual effort. The frequent repetition of single acts of virtue results in the formation of virtuous habits. If, then, I want to bring constant acts of faith, hope, and love into the context of my life, I have to repeat such acts as often as possible. I shall then be sure that God is calling me to his innermost communion of life. "My delights were to be with the children of men" (Prov 8:31 Douay version). I shall spare neither pain nor work to attain this community of life and love as quickly as possible and to remain there permanently.

Goal and Purpose of a Life of Prayer

Now I have found the ideal of my hoping and striving, bursting with energy, shining with dedication, saturated with the blood of sacrifice. Now I know what I want to, can, and should attain. Up until now I lived without a clear-cut goal, and the discomforts of the way made me tired and discouraged. Now, however, I see clearly, I am sure of my way and my goal, and nothing should hold me back from now on. I will not rest until I have found God in the innermost region of my heart. "I found him whom my soul loves. I held him, and would not let him go" (Song 3:4). Love lends me wings, "for love is strong as death" (Song 8:6). I will no longer shrink back from difficulties, for "I can do all things in him who strengthens me" (Phil 4:13).

When I look over my past life, I have to admit that I have made such little progress in the spiritual life because I was lacking in the proper goal.

I didn't understand how greatly our divine Savior was thirsting for souls who would give themselves to him without reserve and to whom he could give himself with the same fullness. The degree of our trust and unity with him is measured by the extent of the generosity with which we follow the invitations of grace. Jesus did not set any limits to his love. He only longs to give himself wholly and to be able to possess souls without any reservations. But souls fear him, since they shy away from the requirements that this intimacy demands of men and women: sacrifice and self-denial.

From now on I shall be honest and upright with myself. I know that God wants to take complete possession of me and that he has predestined me to be transformed into the image of his Son Jesus. He wants me to be his child despite my unworthiness. Who can consider themselves worthy of such favor?

But it is not "in spite of" my unworthiness that God longs for my soul. Rather it is precisely because of my misery that he wants to make me a masterpiece of his love, mercy, and glorification. The more unsuitable the material is, the greater the fame and prowess of the artist, who succeeds despite everything in making a work of art out of it. Our divine Savior wants to bring this truth to us more clearly and help us to grasp it through the parables of the prodigal son and the lost sheep. For there is more joy in heaven over a single converted sinner than over the perseverance of a whole multitude of the just.

Since I have resolved, from now on, to strive for this ideal, I must recognize in all of my thinking, willing, and doing that I am nothing of myself, so that I can give myself over to him with my whole being and all that I have.

The important thing is to believe effectively in his love. "Your faith has made you well" (Lk 8:48).

From Obstacles Come Means

What up until now seemed to me like obstacles, such as temptations, distractions, internal and external difficulties, will now serve as helps to me. When earlier, instead of rising, I always fell deeper through my sins, faults, and weaknesses, I just stayed there. I did not know how to make use of my failings. Now, however, I see that with the grace of God that "fall" can be used to raise me so much more surely to God, and bring me to my goal, just as someone who fears to dive may stay on the diving board, even though it would propel him to his goal; and similarly, what might previously have been a hindrance and source of discouragement to my efforts can now serve as the means for raising me up from creatures to their Creator. In all of this I now recognize a pressing invitation of God to unite myself as closely as possible with him through acts of faith, trust, self-giving, and love. And so everything discouraging is for me a pure grace, which enables and invites me to live more and act more through God and in God.

Haste, fearful self-consciousness, and distraction have till now so often influenced and ruled my life. From now on, however, I shall live with a spirit of trust and of pure abandonment to God's all-knowing and all-gracious providence. Before, nothing so depressed and worried me as my failings and weaknesses, but now I boast of them in the spirit of contrition. "I will all the more gladly boast of my weaknesses, that the power of Christ may rest upon me" (2 Cor 12:9). They should help to convince me of the nothingness of my own ego and move me to let myself be completely filled by Christ, insofar as through the awakening of faith, confidence, and love I unite myself more and more intimately with God. The feelings and desires of the old man must die out. "He must increase, but I must decrease—*Illum*

oportet crescere, me autem minui" (Jn 3:30). The more
I recede, the more will he grow.

So little by little I will overcome the unforeseen
occurrences of life and the petty things of this world
and master them. All of my former enemies are now
helpful to me in moving me closer to my ideal, and they
serve to push me towards ever greater faithfulness and
generosity and to trust that is ever more intimate.

Application to Practical Life

According to what Jesus has said, prayer should expand
to include one's entire day. Let me try to show how that
is possible.

Before beginning all of my activities and works,
and often during them, I should recollect myself for a
moment. Repeating this act accustoms one to greet our
Lord present in his soul as often as possible. And thus,
through his grace, I shall one day reach the point of having him constantly in sight and never forgetting him.

While reading it is enough from time to time, perhaps in the slight interval while turning a page, to direct
one's attention to the center of the soul in order to
maintain and deepen one's connection with God.

The time of relaxation, a walk for example, is not
time lost to one's interior life. I shall stir up some acts of
virtue, to find union with God again or to hold on to it,
and so remain simply, without great effort, in this godly

atmosphere. I connect with God as with a dear friend: even without always speaking with him, I feel happy simply knowing that he is close to me. That is enough.

If we find ourselves in a place in which God is not shown any honor, love, and glory, then we love and honor him there so much the more intimately and with all the more fervor.

At my evening examination of conscience I go through the past day peacefully, checking to see if I was neglectful and have left God in my soul unnoticed for too long a time. In doing so, I discover that I was most troubled with mistakes when my neglect of God was most prolonged. While grace perfects its work in us, let us help it along as much as we can. We strive with human means to bring an intense interior life to fulfillment and further development. Thus, for example we seek through reading and study to penetrate more deeply into the truths of holy Church, especially its lofty teaching about the divine filiation of souls called to participate in divine life.

Above all else, I shall make use of the most excellent means, the holy sacraments. I shall receive them as often as possible and with the greatest possible love and self-surrender. For the sacred humanity of our Savior is the gateway to his divinity. No one comes to God the Father except through Jesus his Son.

In a mysterious way Jesus purifies us from our sins and failures in holy absolution. In the Holy Eucharist he approaches us with his humanity and leads us ever deeper into his divinity. And when the sacramental species are no longer present in us, we can continue our communion, our union with the divinity of our Redeemer, until the next sacramental bonding. Our thanksgiving does not limit itself to a few minutes. With the disciples of Emmaus, we ask our divine Savior after Holy Communion: "Lord, stay with us!" (Lk 24:29). Thus it becomes the unsurpassable source of our inner life: its efficacy expands to our whole day and fills us with ever new zeal.

Let us raise our eyes filled with trust to the loving Mother of God, who is also our mother. She has given us the life of the Redeemer and she will also lead us to supernatural life, until, having grown to maturity in her son Jesus, we reach the perfection of unity with him.

Mary, mother of fairest love, lead us to Jesus!

CHAPTER 3

The Spirit of the Gospel

Our Spiritual Riches

This teaching about the spiritual life, whose foundation and basic elements we have presented in short form and whose development we have depicted, is not new, nor do we mean to present it as such. On the contrary! Anyone who reads the Gospel intelligently can see that this is the way our Savior himself set out for souls.

When people speak about Christianity, and especially about interior life, the principal emphasis is commonly given to the duties and tasks entailed. Too seldom do we hear of its beauty and joy, its hidden splendor, by which God makes those souls who are true to him already happy on this earth. And this despite the fact that the psalmist speaks about this exultant happiness: "They feast on the abundance of thy house, and thou givest them drink from the river of thy delights" (Ps 36:8).

Instead of speaking of what "ought" to be done in the interior life, we need to speak of what, from a supernatural perspective, "is." The point is that God only demands from us what we have and are—that is, very little—while he in exchange gives himself, his eternal life in never-ending bliss. That is clearly expressed in the Gospel.

Sadly, however, many spiritual writers do not mention or discuss the riches promised to us in which every child of God can share through the merits of Christ. How far these writers are from recognizing the true nature of our relationship to God!

The Gospel insists on it as the essential condition for the union of the soul with God that we die to ourselves. God demanded that already from mankind in the Old Testament: "Man shall not see me and live" (Ex 33:20).

With an insistence and imperative no less austere and uncompromising, Jesus declares: "If any man would come after me, let him deny himself and take up his cross and follow me" (Mt 16:24).

Even the strictest ascetics could do nothing other then repeat this demand, while in doing so often misplacing the special accent of the divine teaching. The following of Christ demands the sacrifice of our whole being, a holocaust. The smallest holding back, the slightest tincture of human reckoning and wisdom, is enough to separate us from our master, for he despises a self-giving that is compromised and partial.

"No one who puts his hand to the plow and looks back is fit for the kingdom of God" (Lk 9:62).

"Because you are lukewarm, and neither cold nor hot, I will spew you out of my mouth" (Rev 3:16).

And so our divine Master demands with the strictest exactness, as a requirement of his love, a man's absolute and complete self-surrender. No teacher of human wisdom has ever dared to make this demand.

Then, however, the day will come when my soul goes to God and becomes one with him through an unspeakable grace. "My soul melted when he spoke" (Song 5:6 Douay version). Union with God is from now on the ideal of my soul. I will not rest or be quiet till I have reached this goal. I will make good every lost moment through increased zeal. Faith will become stronger, hope more spirited, and love more ardent.

Jesus' Last Words

But this commandment and insistent advice, which demand with such vehemence that we die to ourselves, are only a part, and in fact the negative part, of the teaching of our Lord. In order to learn his will and thought in their fullness, we must read the fourth Gospel especially. In the accounts of the Synoptic Gospels our Lord speaks a great deal of the time in parables and similes. But in the Gospel of St. John, the beloved disciple, he reveals clearly and openly the purposes of his love and lets us understand why he so rigorously insists on the sacrifice of our poor human life: he wants to replace it with his divine life (chapters 14–17).

One cannot go deeply enough into these pages, which contain the spiritual testament of our Lord. Most of the works of spiritual writers pale beside the boldness and depth of these thoughts and words. Of all spiritual books, the Gospel is the most demanding and makes the highest claims. It is also more sure and all-embracing in its invitation to the supernatural life, more generous and bold in its promises of a union of love with God, than all other mystical works.

In these four chapters of St. John's Gospel our divine Savior unveils and proclaims the deepest secrets of his teaching and no longer speaks in parables and similes. And his disciples finally understand him: "Ah, now you are speaking plainly, not in any figure!" (Jn 16:29). Thus we have to consider the farewell discourse of Jesus and his high priestly prayer as a summary of his whole teaching and as the key to his good news.

The necessity of penance and mortification is expressed in a few verses, which are reminiscent of the admonitions presented in the other Gospels. Love apart from truly following the commandments is excluded. One cannot be a friend and disciple of Jesus if one refuses to carry his cross. The deed is proof of love; love and deed are so closely linked that neither can survive without the other.

"If you love me, you will keep my commandments" (Jn 14:15).

"He who has my commandments and keeps them, he it is who loves me."

"You are my friends if you do what I command you" (Jn 14:21; 15:14).

Our divine Master did not hide from his apostles the suffering and persecution that faced them if they walked the path of abnegation and the following of Christ.

"If you were of the world, the world would love its own; but because you are not of the world . . . therefore the world hates you" (Jn 15:19).

"I have given them thy word; and the world has hated them because they are not of the world, even as I am not of the world" (17–14).

"You will weep and lament, but the world will rejoice" (16–20).

"In the world you have tribulation; but be of good cheer, I have overcome the world" (16:33).

The surest sign by which one can distinguish the chosen from the world, is their obedience towards their divine Master and his commandments.

"Lord, how is it that you will manifest yourself to us, and not to the world?" Jesus answered him, "If a man loves me, he will keep my word" (Jn 14:22–23).

This one word is enough to identify the world and to convict it.

The Promises of the Gospel

Christ wants us to empty our hearts in order to fill them, but only with the divine. The cleansing is and will remain imperfect, as long as it lacks this divine filling as its consequence, just as the divine life cannot unfold in us unless we liberate ourselves from bondage to created things. The death of the ego and life in God are inseparably bound up with one another: one without the other is impossible.

Listen to what Christ promises those who follow his word! These are promises he wants to fulfill for each and every one of us—yes, there is a divine impatience burning in him to make them a reality.

"He who loves me will be loved by my Father, and I will love him and manifest myself to him. . . . We will come to him and make our home with him" (Jn 14:21–23).

"In that day you will know that I am in my Father, and you in me, and I in you" (14:20).

"I will pray the Father, and he will give you another Counselor, to be with you forever, even the Spirit of truth . . . he dwells with you, and will be in you" (14:16–17).

This reciprocal indwelling, this merger, this "astonishing union" (*The Imitation of Christ*) with the three divine Persons is the exalted goal that should be set before the eyes of souls at the very beginning of their spiritual life. It is the express wish and desire of our Lord himself. It is not enough to try to inspire souls regarding a heavenly goal: one must have them to enter the Kingdom of God itself and show them that even here [on earth] this is their portion and possession: "The kingdom of God is within you" (Lk 17:21 Douay).

Outside of this union with Christ our Lord and the trusting relationship with the Father and the Holy Spirit arising from it, there is neither any truly deep spiritual life nor any supernatural fruitfulness.

"Abide in me, and I in you. As the branch cannot bear fruit by itself, unless it abides in the vine, neither can you, unless you abide in me."

"I am the vine, you are the branches. He who abides in me, and I in him, he it is that bears much fruit, for apart from me you can do nothing."

"If a man does not abide in me, he is cast forth as a branch and withers; and the branches are gathered, thrown into the fire and burned."

"If you abide in me, and my words abide in you, ask whatever you will, and it shall be done for you" (Jn 15:4–8)

The quiet prayer of souls united to Christ, who live in the fullness of his life, has sovereign power and meaning. Where once the soul devoted itself only to making requests and giving thanks, now its prayer is in ceaseless, resonant harmony with the prayer of Christ, which is God's will alone. "In that day you will ask nothing of me. . . . If you ask anything of the Father, he will give it to you in my name" (Jn 17:23).

"I do not say to you that I shall pray to the Father for you; for the Father himself loves you, because you have loved me and have believed that I came from the Father" (Jn 16:26–27).

A soul that has fully assimilated God's word, taking it into itself as the Holy Virgin did, will become like her, a seat of Wisdom. She is illuminated by divine light.

To such a soul, in which he would dwell with the Father and the Holy Spirit, our Lord expressly promised this gift of which the world knows nothing.

"The Counselor, the Holy Spirit, whom the Father will send in my name, he will teach you all things, and bring to your remembrance all that I have said to you" (Jn 14:26).

"No longer do I call you servants, for the servant does not know what his master is doing; but I have called you friends, for all that I have heard from my Father I have made known to you" (Jn 15:15).

"When the Spirit of truth comes, he will guide you into all the truth" (Jn 16:13).

This awareness is eternal life that already has begun here in this world of time and space. "This is eternal life, that they know thee the only true God, and Jesus Christ whom thou hast sent" (Jn 17:3).

This knowledge is not just a theoretical, abstract science, but a realized wisdom, translated into act and life: filled with love, goodness, mercy, and mildness.

Powerful streams of divine love saturate the soul that is true to it, in order to stream out to countless other souls and then to return again to their source. The more this love of God who is truly present to us grows in generosity and intimacy, the more the soul is irradiated by an ever-growing, deep insight which in turn increases its love.

"Abide in my love!" (Jn 15:9).

When intellect, will, and imagination are purified in this way and brought back to their divine origins, when the soul is captured by the divine life and brought into it, then it knows true happiness. "These things I have spoken to you, that my joy may be in you, and that your joy may be full" (Jn 15:11).

"Your sorrow will turn into joy" (Jn 16:20).

"Your hearts will rejoice, and no one will take your joy from you" (Jn 16:22).

"I have said this to you, that in me you may have peace. . . . Peace I leave with you; my peace I give to you" (Jn 16:33, 14:27).

In the luminous simplicity and security of a life that has been divinized through and through, the soul rejoices with an indescribable peace.

It experiences the fulfillment of the last words of the high priestly prayer of Jesus:

"That they may all be one; even as thou, Father, art in me, and I in thee, that they also may be in us, so that the world may believe that thou hast sent me.

"The glory which thou hast given me I have given
to them, that they may be one even as we are one, I in
them and thou in me, that they may become perfectly
one, so that the world may know that thou hast sent
me and hast loved them even as thou hast loved me"
(Jn 17:21–23).

Notes

Notes

Notes

Notes

Notes

Notes

Notes

Notes